GUITAR TAB EDITION

MW00700014

ACOUSTIC ROCK CLASSICS

A No-Nonsense Approach to Playing 10 of Your Favorite Songs

About the TNT Changer

Use the TNT software to change keys, loop playback, and mute tracks for play-along. For complete instructions, see the TnT ReadMe.pdf file on your enhanced CD.

Windows users: insert the CD into your computer, double-click on My Computer, right-click on your CD drive icon, and select Explore to locate the file.

Mac users: insert the CD into your computer and double-click on the CD icon on your desktop to locate the file.

Produced by
Alfred Music Publishing Co., Inc.
P.O. Box 10003
Van Nuys, CA 91410-0003
alfred.com

Printed in USA.

Cover photo: Guitarist © Dreamstime.com / Michael Flippo

Recordings: Chauncey Gardiner Combo, featuring
Erick Lynen on vocals

ISBN-10: 0-7390-6901-2 (Book & CD)
ISBN-13: 978-0-7390-6901-1 (Book & CD)

 Alfred Cares. Contents printed on 100% recycled paper.

Contents

* For minus-vocals and minus-guitar versions, use the TNT software.

BLACK WATER

Acous. Gtr. 1 in Dbl. Drop D tuning:
⑥ = D ③ = G
⑤ = A ② = B
④ = D ① = D

Words and Music by
PATRICK SIMMONS

Moderately slow ♩ = 84

Intro:

Am7(4) D5 Am7(4) D5

Acous. Gtr. 1 Rhy. Fig. 1

mf
fingerstyle

end Rhy. Fig. 1

Am7(4) D5 Am7(4) D5

1. Well, I've

Verse:
w/Rhy. Fig. 1 *(Acous. Gtr. 1) cont. simile, 4 times*

Am7(4) D5 Am7(4) D5 Am7(4) D5

built me a raft___ and she's read - y for float - in'; ol' Mis - sis - sip - pi,___ she's
2. *See additional lyrics*

Am7(4) D5 Am7(4) D5 Am7(4) D5

call - in' my name._ Cat - fish are jump - in', that pad - dle wheel thump - in', black

Black Water - 5 - 1

Guitar Solo:

w/Rhy. Fig. 1 *(Acous. Gtr. 1) cont. simile, 5 times*

Outro:

w/Rhy. Fig. 1 *(Acous. Gtr. 1) cont. simile till fade*

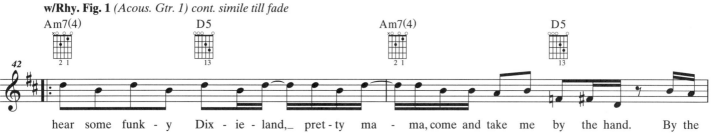

hear some funk - y Dix - ie - land, __ pret - ty ma - ma, come and take me by the hand. By the

*Acous. Gtr. 1 fades out and then fades back in.

Repeat ad lib. and fade

hand, take me by the hand, pret - ty ma - ma, come and dance with your dad - dy all __ night long. I'd like to

Verse 2:
Well, if it rains, I don't care,
Don't make no difference to me;
Just take that streetcar that's goin' uptown.
Yeah, I'd like to hear some funky
Dixieland and dance a honky-tonk,
And I'll be buyin' everybody drinks all 'round.
(To Chorus:)

CAT'S IN THE CRADLE

Capo 8th fret to match recording.

Words and Music by
HARRY CHAPIN and SANDY CHAPIN

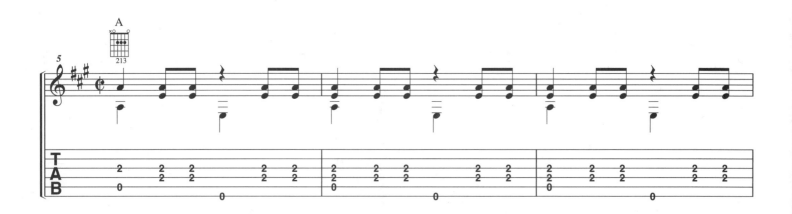

𝄋 *Verses 1–3:*

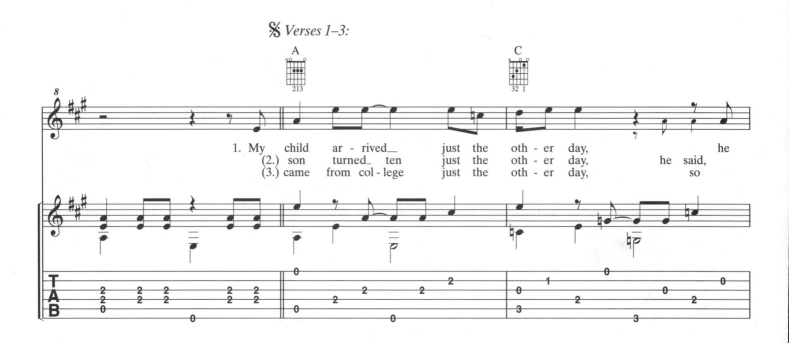

1. My child ar - rived__ just the oth - er day, he
(2.) son turned__ ten just the oth - er day, he said,
(3.) came from col - lege just the oth - er day, so

Cat's in the Cradle - 6 - 1

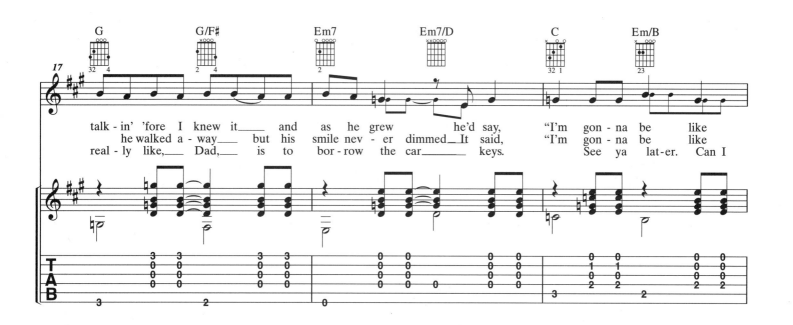

you, Dad. You know I'm gon-na be like you."}
him, yeah. You know I'm gon-na be like him."}

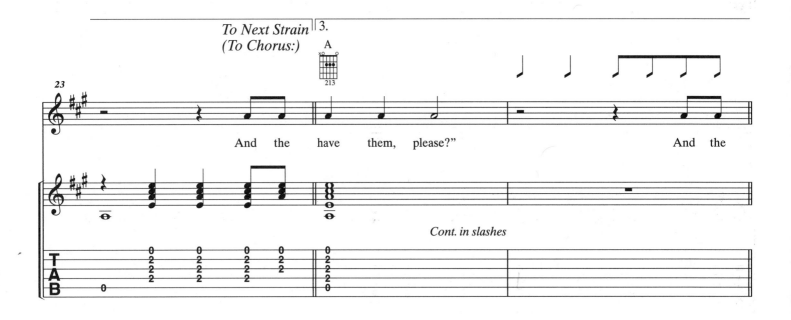

To Next Strain
(To Chorus:)

And the have them, please?" And the

Cont. in slashes

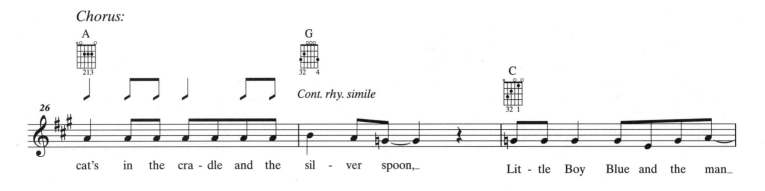

Chorus:

Cont. rhy. simile

cat's in the cra-dle and the sil - ver spoon,_ Lit - tle Boy Blue and the man_

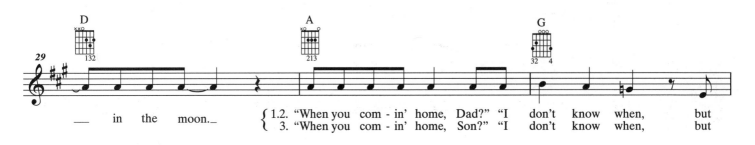

___ in the moon._ { 1.2. "When you com - in' home, Dad?" "I don't know when, but
{ 3. "When you com - in' home, Son?" "I don't know when, but

12

Chorus:

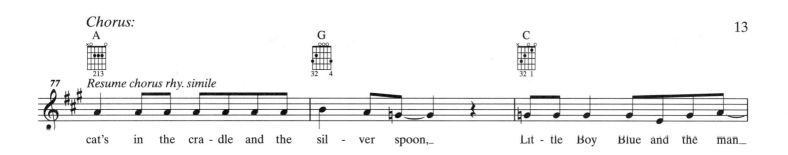

cat's in the cra - dle and the sil - ver spoon,__ Lit - tle Boy Blue and the man__

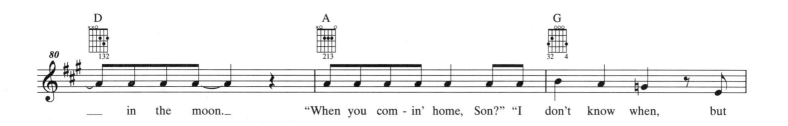

__ in the moon.__ "When you com - in' home, Son?" "I don't know when, but

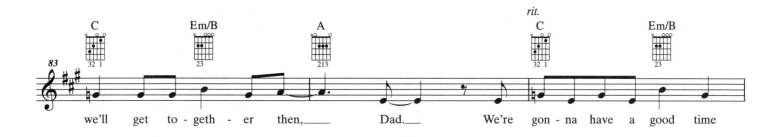

we'll get to - geth - er then,___ Dad.__ We're gon - na have a good time

Outro:

Slower ♩ = 58

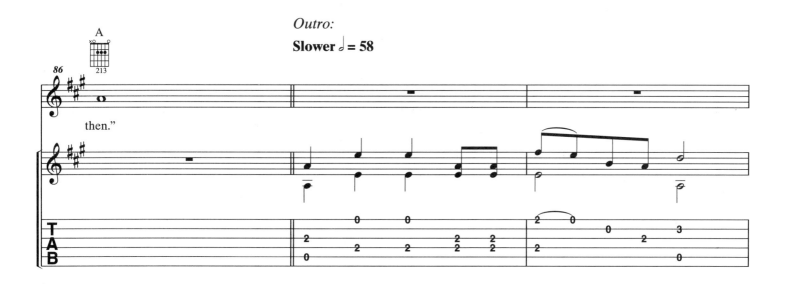

then."

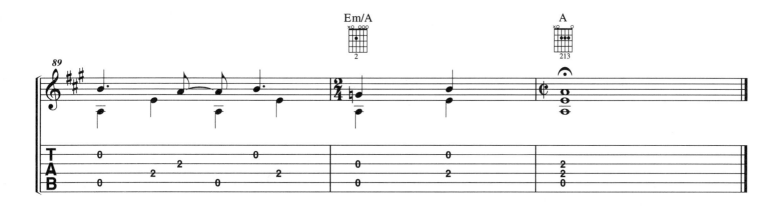

FOR WHAT IT'S WORTH
(There's Something Happening Here)

Words and Music by
STEPHEN STILLS

For What It's Worth - 2 - 1

Verse 2:
There's battle lines being drawn,
Nobody's right if everybody's wrong.
Young people speaking their minds,
Getting so much resistance from behind.
I think it's time we stop,…
(To Chorus:)

Verse 3:
What a field day for the heat,
A thousand people in the street.
Singing songs and carrying signs,
Mostly say, "Hooray for our side."
It's time we stop,…
(To Chorus:)

Verse 4:
Paranoia strikes deep,
Into your life it will creep.
It starts when you're always afraid,
Step out of line, the man come and take you away.
We better stop,…
(To Chorus:)

LAYLA
(*Unplugged* version)

Words and Music by
ERIC CLAPTON and JIM GORDON

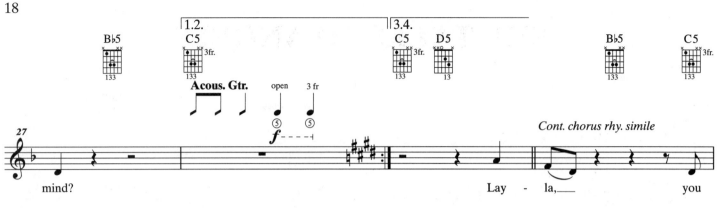

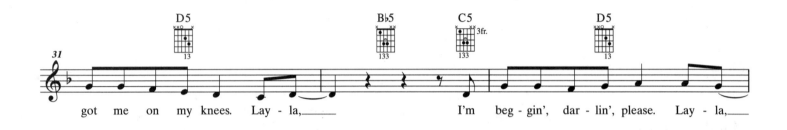

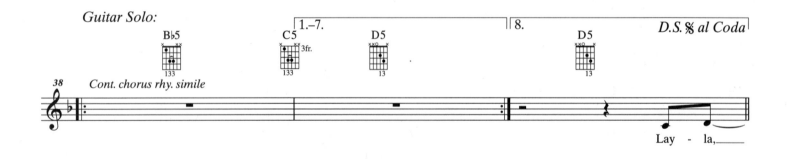

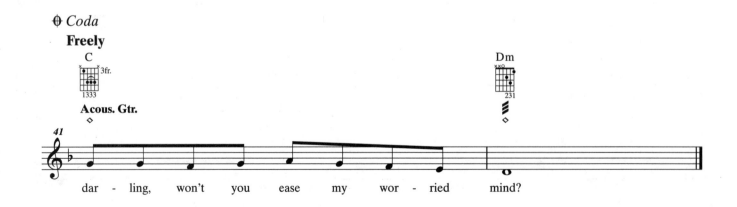

SHE TALKS TO ANGELS

Gtr. tuned in Open E:

⑥ = E ③ = G
⑤ = B ② = B
④ = E ① = E

Words and Music by
CHRIS ROBINSON and RICH ROBINSON

Slow ballad ♩ = 80

*A6/9 chord occurs as an embellishment on every occurance of Rhy. Fig. 1.

She Talks to Angels - 5 - 1

20

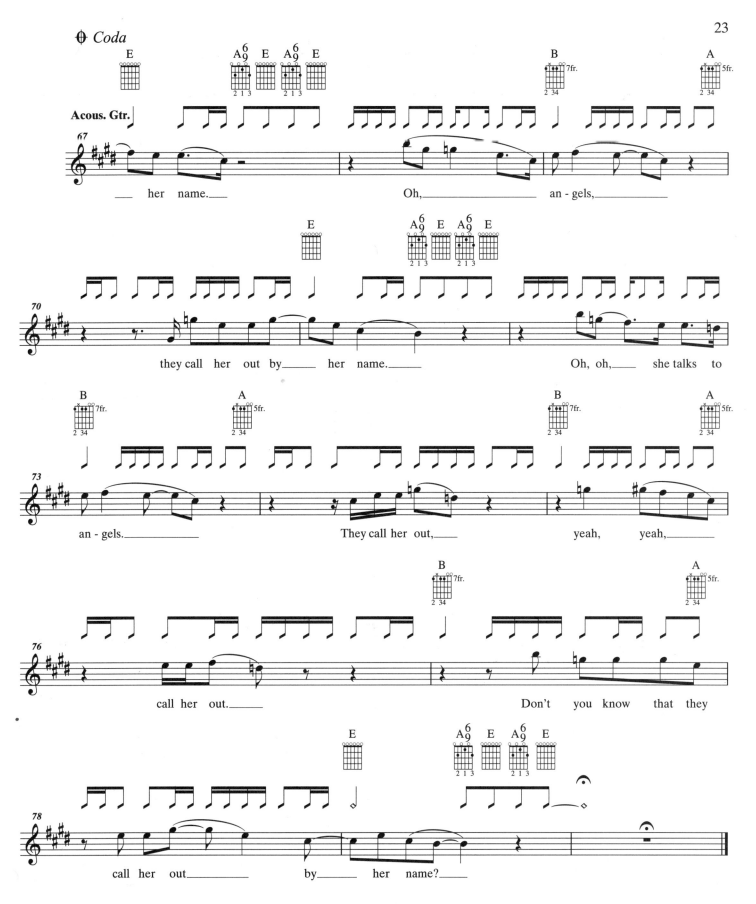

Verse 3:
She keeps a lock of hair in her pocket.
She wears a cross around her neck.
The hair is from a little boy,
And the cross from someone she has not met.
Well, not yet.
(To Chorus:)

Verse 4:
Repeat Verse 2

MELISSA

Words and Music by
STEVE ALAIMO and
GREGG ALLMAN

Verse 2:
Freight train, each car looks the same, all the same.
And no one knows the gypsy's name,
No one hears his lonely sigh.
There are no blankets where he lies.
In all his deepest dreams, the gypsy flies
With sweet Melissa.

Verse 3:
Crossroads, will you ever let him go? (Lord, Lord).
Will you hide the dead man's ghost?
Or will he lie beneath the clay?
Or will his spirit float away?
But I know that he won't stay
Without Melissa.
(To Coda)

Melissa - 4 - 4

SISTER GOLDEN HAIR

Words and Music by
GERRY BECKLEY

TAKE IT EASY

Words and Music by
JACKSON BROWNE
and GLENN FREY

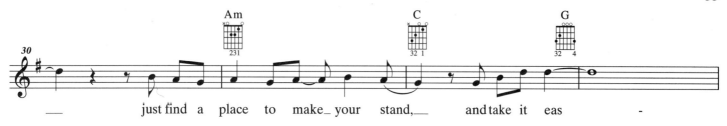

just find a place to make your stand, and take it eas -

y. 2.Well, I'm a - y.

Guitar Solo:

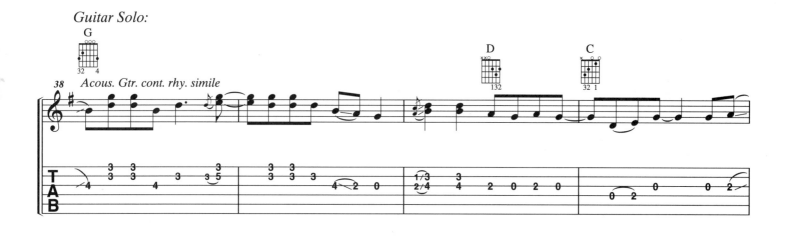

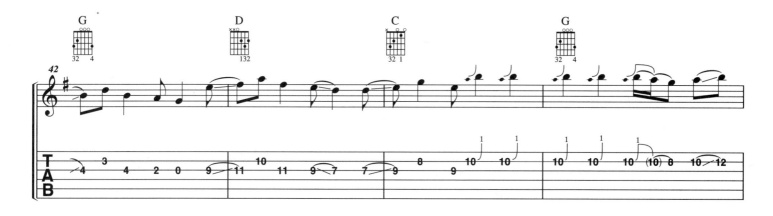

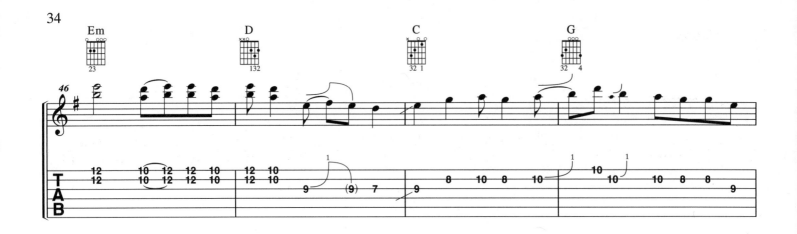

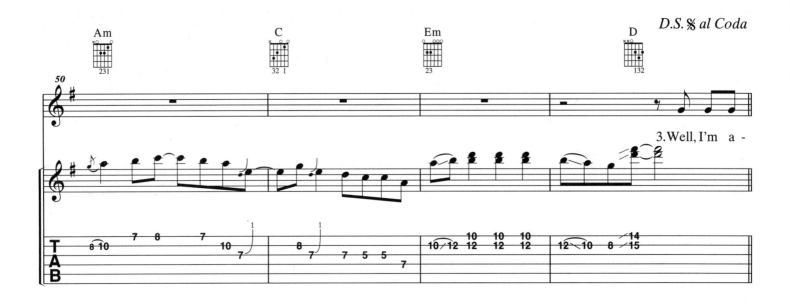

D.S. ℅ al Coda

3. Well, I'm a -

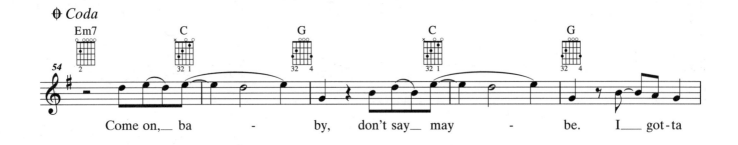

Come on,__ ba - by, don't say__ may - be. I__ got-ta

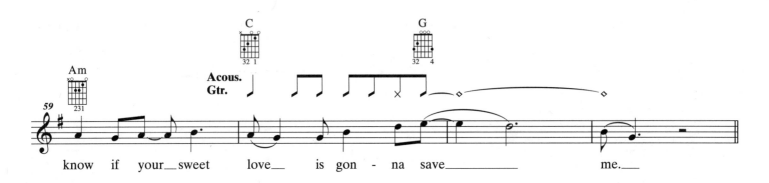

know if your__sweet love__ is gon - na save_____ me.__

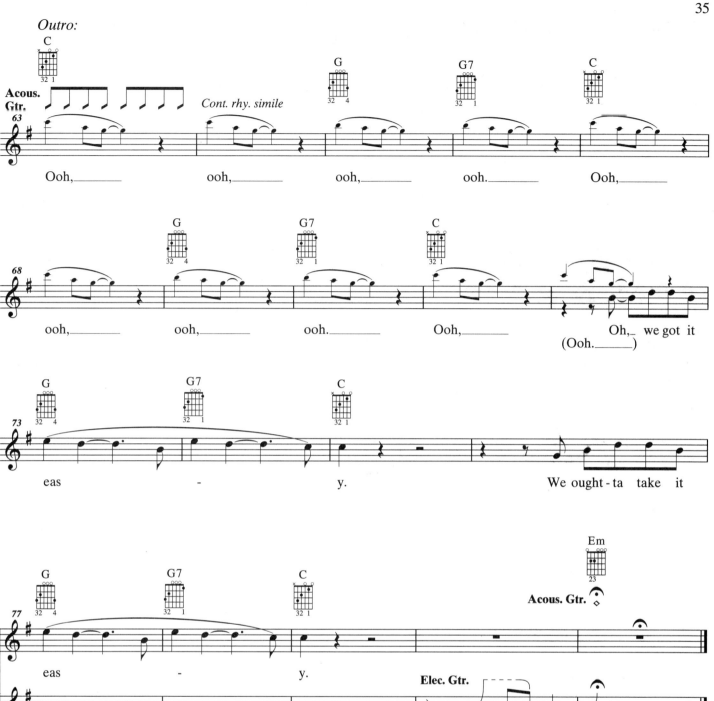

Verse 2:
Well, I'm a-standin' on a corner in Winslow, Arizona,
And such a fine sight to see:
It's a girl, my Lord, in a flatbed Ford
Slowin' down to take a look at me.

Chorus 2:
Come on, baby, don't say maybe.
I gotta know if your sweet love is gonna save me.
We may lose and we may win,
Though we will never be here again.
So open up, I'm climbin' in, so take it easy.
(To Guitar Solo:)

Verse 3:
Well, I'm a-runnin' down the road, tryin' to loosen my load,
Got a world of trouble on my mind.
Lookin' for a lover who won't blow my cover,
She's so hard to find.
(To Chorus:)

WISH YOU WERE HERE

Words and Music by
ROGER WATERS and DAVID GILMOUR

Slow ♩ = 60

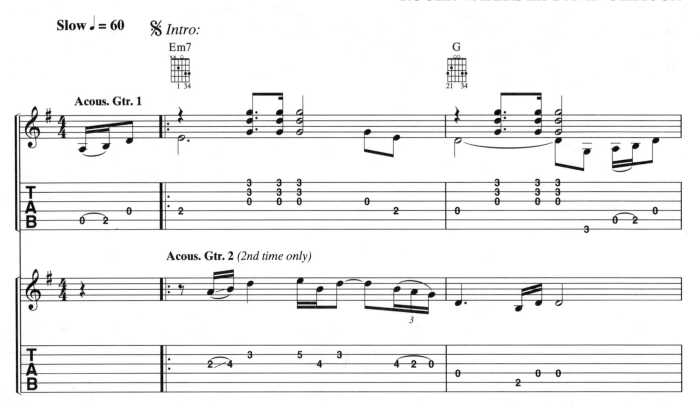

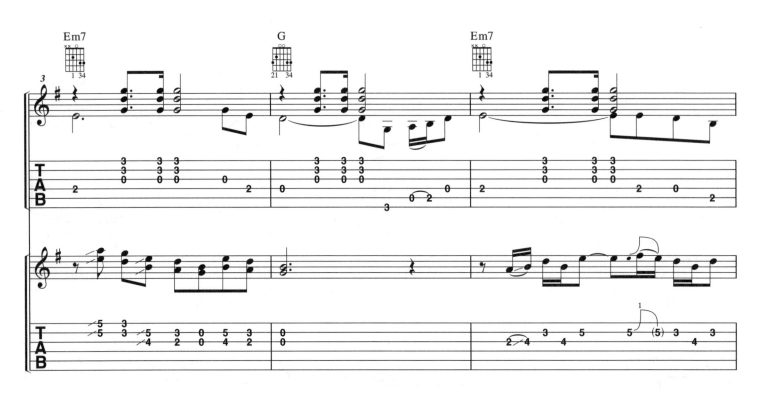

Wish You Were Here - 4 - 1

Verse 2:
How I wish,
How I wish you were here.
We're just two lost souls
Swimming in a fish bowl,
Year after year.
Running over the same ground,
What have we found?
The same old fears,
Wish you were here.

YOU CAN'T ALWAYS GET WHAT YOU WANT

Words and Music by
MICK JAGGER and KEITH RICHARDS

Moderately slow ♩ = 82

(gradual accelerando throughout)

Intro:

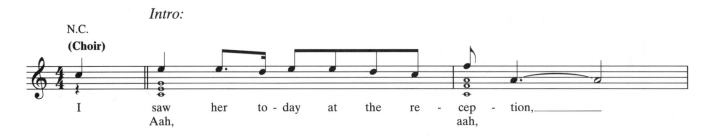

I saw her to-day at the re - cep - tion,_____
Aah,   aah,

a glass of wine____ in her hand._____   I knew she would meet her con -
aah,   aah.   Aah,

nec - tion,_____ at her feet was a foot - loose man.__   No, you
aah,   aah,   aah.

can't al - ways get what you want.__   You can't al - ways get what you want.__   You
Aah,   aah,   aah,   aah.

can't al - ways get what you want.__   And if you try some - time_____ you'll
Aah,   aah,   aah,

You Can't Always Get What You Want - 7 - 1

*Acous. Gtr. capo VIII, in Open E tuning: ⑥ = E; ⑤ = B; ④ = E; ③ = G♯; ② = B; ① = E
(Chord frames and TAB numbers relative to capo.)
**Chord frames reflect capoed gtr. (Chords in parenthesis reflect concert key).

% Verses 1, 2, 4, & 5:

saw her to-day_ at the re-cep - tion, a glass of wine_ in her hand.
2.4.5. See additional lyrics

enter on Verse 2, ad lib. simile on repeats

*Elec. Gtr. in standard tuning w/o capo (TAB numbers are as written).

44

Chorus:

Outro: *Repeat ad lib. and fade*

TABLATURE EXPLANATION

TAB illustrates the six strings of the guitar.
Notes and chords are indicated by the placement of fret numbers on each string.

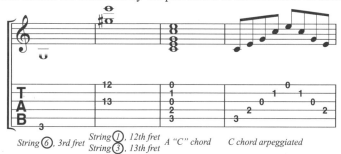

String ⑥, 3rd fret   String ①, 12th fret   A "C" chord   C chord arpeggiated
                      String ③, 13th fret

BENDING NOTES

Half Step:
Play the note and bend string one half step (one fret).

Whole Step:
Play the note and bend string one whole step (two frets).

Slight Bend/ Quarter-Tone Bend:
Play the note and bend string sharp.

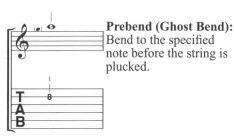

Prebend (Ghost Bend):
Bend to the specified note before the string is plucked.

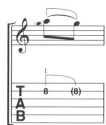

Prebend and Release:
Play the already-bent string, then immediately drop it down to the fretted note.

Unison Bends:
Play both notes and immediately bend the lower note to the same pitch as the higher note.

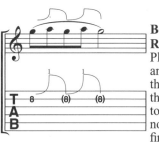

Bend and Release:
Play the note and bend to the next pitch, then release to the original note. Only the first note is attacked.

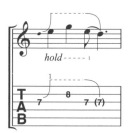

Bends Involving More Than One String:
Play the note and bend the string while playing an additional note on another string. Upon release, relieve the pressure from the additional note allowing the original note to sound alone.

Bends Involving Stationary Notes:
Play both notes and immediately bend the lower note up to pitch. Return as indicated.

ARTICULATIONS

Hammer On:
Play the lower note, then "hammer" your finger to the higher note. Only the first note is plucked.

Pull Off:
Play the higher note with your first finger already in position on the lower note. Pull your finger off the first note with a strong downward motion that plucks the string— sounding the lower note.

Legato Slide:
Play the first note and, keeping pressure applied on the string, slide up to the second note. The diagonal line shows that it is a slide and not a hammer-on or a pull-off.

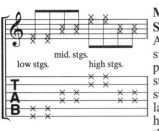

Muted Strings:
A percussive sound is produced by striking the strings while laying the fret hand across them.

Palm Mute:
The notes are muted (muffled) by placing the palm of the pick hand lightly on the strings, just in front of the bridge.

HARMONICS

Natural Harmonic:
A finger of the fret hand lightly touches the string at the note indicated in the TAB and is plucked by the pick producing a bell-like sound called a harmonic.

RHYTHM SLASHES

Strum Marks/ Rhythm Slashes:
Strum with the indicated rhythm pattern. Strum marks can be located above the staff or within the staff.

Single Notes with Rhythm Slashes:
Sometimes single notes are incorporated into a strum pattern. The circled number below is the string and the fret number is above.

Artificial Harmonic:
Fret the note at the first TAB number, lightly touch the string at the fret indicated in parens (usually 12 frets higher than the fretted note), then pluck the string with an available finger or your pick.

TREMOLO BAR

Specified Interval:
The pitch of a note or chord is lowered to the specified interval and then return as indicated. The action of the tremolo bar is graphically represented by the peaks and valleys of the diagram.

Unspecified Interval:
The pitch of a note or chord is lowered, usually very dramatically, until the pitch of the string becomes indeterminate.

PICK DIRECTION

Downstrokes and Upstrokes:
The downstroke is indicated with this symbol (⊓) and the upstroke is indicated with this (∨).